50 Chair Exercises For Seniors

Best Chair Workout For Older Adults To Build Strength, Balance, Flexibility, Joint Health, Improved Mobility, Pain Relief, and Injury Prevention

Darcy Willis

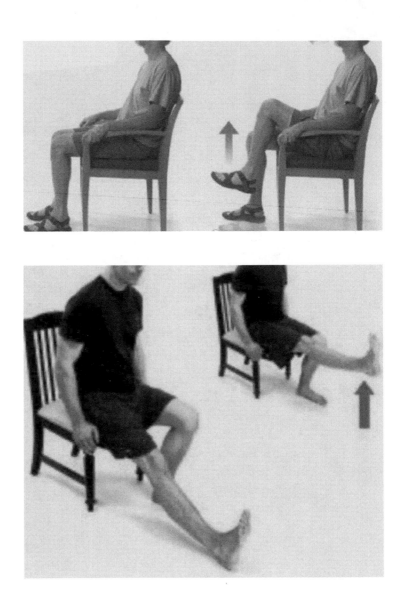

Table of Contents

Introduction

The aging process can be challenging, particularly for those dealing with health and medical issues such as loss of (or deteriorating) hearing and vision, osteoporosis, lack of mobility, and heart disease. These problems can have a significant impact on one's quality of life, resulting in pain, falls, depression, and other ailments.

Although basic exercise routines can ease (and even alleviate) some of the health problems faced by older adults, many people are unable to complete traditional workouts. However, chair exercises can be a very great substitute, allowing individuals to exercise for balance, flexibility, and strength.

Part 1

Getting Started With Chair Exercises For Seniors

Ready to begin sitting exercise? All you need is a chair and a positive attitude!

Ideal Chair

Choose a comfortable chair. The ideal chair will be stable and have a straight back. Wheels are not allowed. The rolling chairs should be left in the office. You will want a chair with a comfy cushion, but not one that is so deep that you will disappear. A strong kitchen chair is an excellent choice.

When To Consider Chair Exercises For Seniors

Chair exercises are great for seniors who want to improve their health and mobility. Any workout demands significant physical effort, but doing it while seated can lessen the amount of strain on your body. This reduces the likelihood of sustaining an injury during the process.

Seated workouts for seniors are very helpful for older persons who have special needs or experiences in their lives.

If you fit into any of the following categories, you should consider implementing some or all of these workouts.

- Struggle to maintain your balance

- Increased fall risk

- Limited mobility

- Recently injured or had surgery

- Just getting into a regular exercise routine

- Wanting to complete daily activities with greater ease

Part 2

Benefits of Seated Chair Exercises for Seniors

The benefits of doing workouts while seated in a chair are numerous. Here are a few of the benefits for seniors.

Easier To Handle For Those With Mobility Or Balance Issues

Standing workouts might be dangerous if you have poor balance or mobility. While it's essential to perform standing exercises to develop your balance & mobility, you may require a safer movement alternative if you're training alone or just beginning to lift weights. Benefit from weight training without risking injury by performing exercises while seated.

Increase Lean Muscle

By the age of 70, the majority of people lose 25% of their valuable muscle mass. Fortunately, seated exercises, especially those that involve resistance bands or dumbbells, are among your best options for restoring any muscle mass you may have lost. Adding strength can also make daily tasks like carrying heavy items and getting out of a chair much simpler.

Increase Blood Circulation

Seated workouts stimulate your muscles and tissues while also pumping blood and other fluids through your limbs. It is really important to increase blood flow, particularly as we become older and spend more time sitting down. Your heart will be put to the test during strength training, which helps to promote cardiovascular health.

Improve Joint Health

Your joints are more likely to self-lubricate when you move your limbs while lifting weights. This will greatly increase the range of motion while lowering stiffness & other joint discomforts. Always keep moving; it's good for you!

Prevent Bone Fractures

Osteoporosis, which can lead to broken bones, is a common sign of getting old. Building your bone strength through exercising your muscles with seated workouts will help you avoid painful fractures in the future.

How Often & How Long Should the Elderly Exercise?

How Often

Consistency is the cornerstone of a productive workout routine. Ideally, you should engage in some form of chair workout every day, or at least very frequently. Aim for 150 minutes a week of moderate, heart-pumping exercise, but split it up whichever works best if doing so every day is unrealistic. Muscle gain also requires consistency and regularity in training. Seniors should do strength exercises twice a week at a minimum.

How Long

Chair workouts or other mild activities should be gradually increased to 30-minute exercises. And if you can't spare 30 minutes all at once, split it up into two 15-minute sessions or three ten-minute workouts. Most elderly people benefit from two 30-minute sessions of muscle-strengthening exercise per week. However, research suggests that even 15 minutes of moderate-intensity exercise may help avoid cardiovascular disease.

Part 3

Preventing Injury Is The Top Priority

It is still possible to slip out of a chair and sustain an injury; therefore, it is crucial to ensure that your elderly loved one is stable in their chair and capable of performing these exercises.

Especially when beginning a new workout routine, remind them to start cautiously and build up their strength gradually.

Until you're sure they can perform the exercises without injury, you should remain nearby while they do them.

Consult a Doctor

Please see a doctor before beginning any of these workouts if:

- Had surgery just recently

- Have any recent injuries that could be worse by overuse of a muscle or group of muscles

- Is unable to maintain the ideal posture when exercising (even the slightest difference to the correct form of each exercise could result in pain or further injury)

This is not a universal check-off list that we're providing. Injuries can make certain workouts more difficult, and they may even require that they be avoided entirely. A senior should not be pressured into performing an exercise if the pain is too great, either immediately or over time. When this happens, the person should quit the activity and find a more relaxed position.

If you are a caregiver for an elderly person and you are unsure of whether or not you are legally allowed to perform any of the following exercises, you should prioritize safety.

Stretching For Seniors

Chair exercises, such as stretching, are ideal for seniors because they can be modified to accommodate a variety of physical limitations, reduce the likelihood of injury from falls, and yet provide health benefits.

A comfortable, nonslip chair is all that is required.

Stretching not only helps relieve aches and pains in the muscles and joints, but also increases mobility, flexibility, coordination, and blood flow.

In addition to its positive effects on the body, it also helps relieve tension and elevates mood.

Part 4

50 Chair Exercises For Seniors

Arm/Shoulder Exercises For Seniors
Shoulders

Shoulders serve a very wide variety of functions for humans. Several common daily activities involve our shoulders, including carrying heavy items, sleeping on them, falling on them, leaning on them, and raising and lowering our arms. Training our shoulders greatly improves our ability when using our arms.

The inability of an elderly person to move their shoulders freely or even partially can lead to weakness, pain in other areas of the body that must compensate, and a general inability to carry out daily tasks.

Shoulder Press With Band

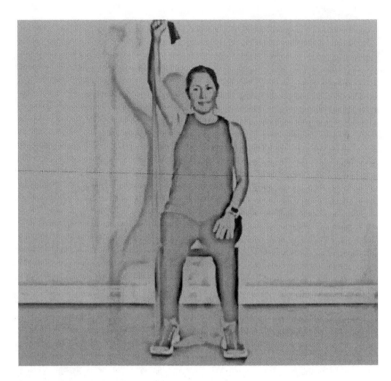

Difficulty: Easy

Sets/Reps: 3/5

Time: 4 Minutes

Instructions:

- Sit tall on a chair

- Step on the band with your right foot.

- Put some tension on the band by holding it with your right hand above your shoulder.

- Throw a fist upwards in an attempt to reach the ceiling.

- Perform 5 repetitions.

- Switch to the left side and repeat

Seated Shoulder Press

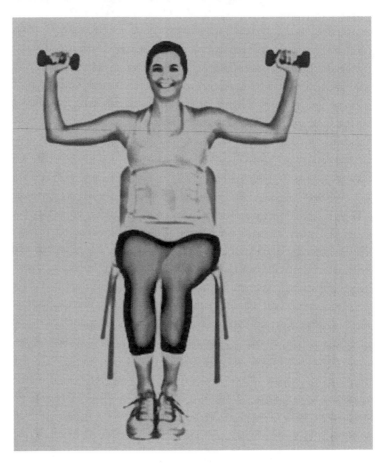

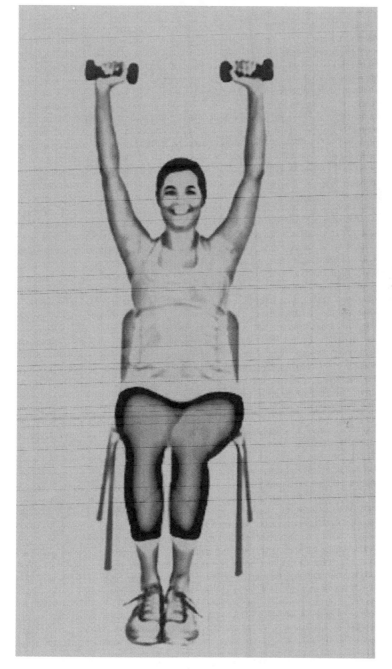

Difficulty: Easy

Sets/Reps: 3/12

Time: 4 Minutes

The seated shoulder press will improve strength, mobility, & endurance while assisting in raising the arms overhead.

Instructions:

Select a set of light dumbbells or a resistance band and slide it under the seat, then sit on it while maintaining an even length on both sides of the body.

- Sit in a chair comfortably with your hips back.

- Be sure your back is properly supported by the chair's backrest.

- Maintain a tight core by contracting the abs & the lumbar.

- To begin, spread your elbows to the sides of your body and bring them beneath your shoulders. Put your chest out.

- Hold the dumbbells in a straight line with the body, palms facing forward.

- Raise your hands while reaching over the head till they are fully stretched out.

- Avoid touching the palms of your hands together, and make sure that both of your arms are held in a parallel position.

- When a full extension is achieved, gradually lower the hands back to the initial position while keeping your elbow spread out.

- Extend your elbows until you feel a pinching sensation (not pain) at your shoulder blades. Avoid tucking your elbows in toward the center of your body.

Seated Front Shoulder Raises

Difficulty: Easy

Sets/Reps: 3/12

Time: 4 Minutes

This is a great way to improve your strength and flexibility for reaching forward or holding an object in front of you.

Instructions:

- Hold a pair of resistance bands, medicine balls, or dumbbells.

- Sit in a chair comfortably with your hips back.

- Be sure your back is properly supported by the chair's backrest.

- Maintain a tight core by contracting the abs & the lumbar. Extend your chest out.

- When lifting dumbbells, your arms should be at your sides, hanging naturally. Your palms should face inward.

- Slide the band under the chair seat or sit down on it, till the length are equal on both sides of your body.

- Then, rest your arms at your sides and let them hang loosely with your palms facing in.

- When using a medicine ball, position the ball so that it is resting on the edge of the lap. With both hands, maintain a firm grasp on the ball while keeping the other hand on each side.

- Continue to raise your arms in front of your body while maintaining your arm straightness and palms facing forward.

- Hold at the point when the hands are parallel to the ground & the arms are within the line of sight of the eyes.

- Proceed by gradually reversing your current position back to the original one.

Seated Knee-to-Elbow

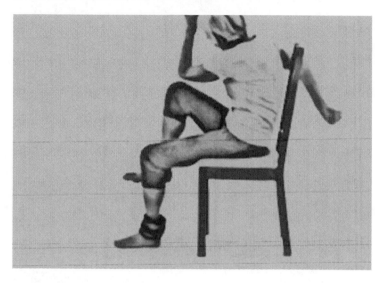

Difficulty:

Sets/Reps: 3/12

Time: 4 Minutes

Instructions:

- Sit comfortably in a chair, Feet firmly planted on the floor.
- Put your hands together at the back of your head, elbows apart.

- Rotate your body to the right & raise the right knee to touch the left elbow.

- To perform the same exercise on the other side, simply turn to the left after returning to the beginning position. Repeat for reps.

Seated Dumbbell Biceps Curls

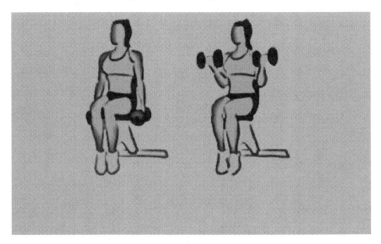

Difficulty: Easy

Sets/Reps: 3/12

Time: 6 Minutes

Instructions:

- Comfortably sit on a chair with a straight back while holding a dumbbell in both hands.

- Hang by the side at arm's length with your palms facing forward

- Keep your arms firmly at your side, then bend the elbows while curling the dumbbells to the shoulder.

- Carefully bring the weight down till your hands are straight. Repeat.

Seated Dumbbell Rows

Difficulty: Medium

Sets/Reps: 3/8

Time: 5 Minutes

Instructions:

- Sit comfortably in a chair. Hold a dumbbell in both hands by your side with your palms facing each other

- Slightly bend forward at your hip. Your elbows should be close to your body. Now squeeze the shoulder blades together to drive the elbow till the upper arms are almost parallel to the ground.

- Carefully return to your beginning position. And repeat

Seated Dumbbell Overhead Shoulder Press

Difficulty: Medium

Sets/Reps: 3/8

Time: 5 Minutes

Instructions:

- Sit comfortably in a chair with a straight back. Raise your arms into a goal post position, with your elbows lifted, and a pair of weights at your sides.

- Pull in your abs and carefully press the dumbbells up till your hands are straight.

- Carefully and slowly bring yourself back to the original posture. Perform the required number of repetitions.

Seated Dumbbell Triceps Kickbacks

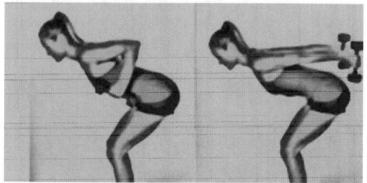

Difficulty: Medium

Sets/Reps: 3/8

Time: 5 Minutes

Instructions:

- In a seated position, bend forward till your chest is nearly parallel to the thighs.

- Hold dumbbells at your sides and bend your arms to the back.

- Make sure your back is flat & your elbows are hugging your sides, now push both dumbbells back till your hands are straight.

- With control, return the arms to your side. Repeat.

Bicep Curl With Band

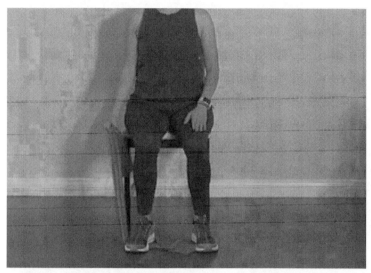

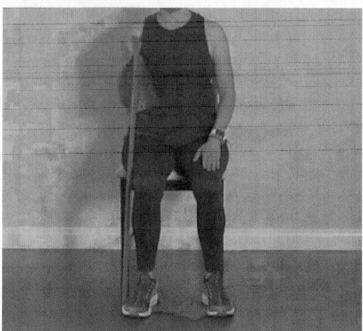

Difficulty: Easy

Sets/Reps: 3/5

Time: 5 Minutes

Instructions:

- Sit tall on a chair

- Plant your right foot firmly on the band.

- Assume a starting position with the band held in your right hand (palm up) until you can feel some resistance.

- Bring your hand up to your shoulder and you'll feel your biceps contract.

- Straighten your arm

- Perform 5 repetitions.

- Repeat on the left.

Chest Exercises For Seniors
Seated Chest Press

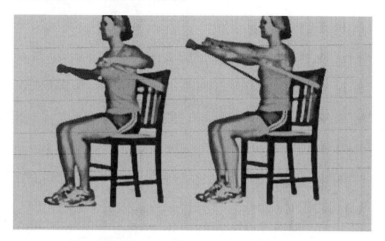

Difficulty: Easy

Sets/Reps: 3/12

Time: 4 Minutes

By simultaneously engaging many muscular groups (chest, shoulders, & triceps), the bench press is considered a compound exercise.

Instructions:

- Hold the resistance band.

- Set the band on the chair so that it lies directly behind your back, just below your shoulder blades.

- Make sure the band cannot move while being used on the chair's back; doing so could cause an injury or cause the workout to focus on the incorrect muscles.

- Consider using a sturdy pin or clip to keep it in place, or have a member of the senior's family assist them in installing a pair of shelving brackets to the back of the chair so that the band remains in the appropriate position.

- Sit comfortably with your hips far back. Be sure your back is properly supported by the chair's backrest.

- Hold your abs and low back in. Put your chest out.

- Keep your palms down & your elbows bent so that they are parallel to your shoulders at all times. Put your hands outside of your shoulders.

- When your arms are fully stretched in front of your body, but not touching, push the resistance band forward.

- With caution, return to the original starting location.

- You can also wrap the band around a post or a beam if you don't have access to a chair that can be adapted for the resistance band.

Seated Bicep Curls

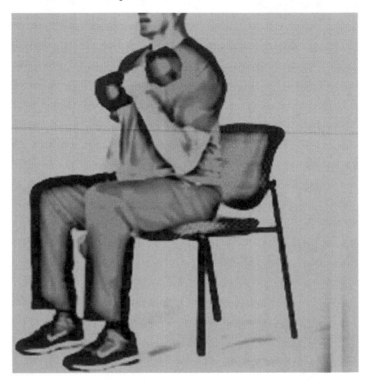

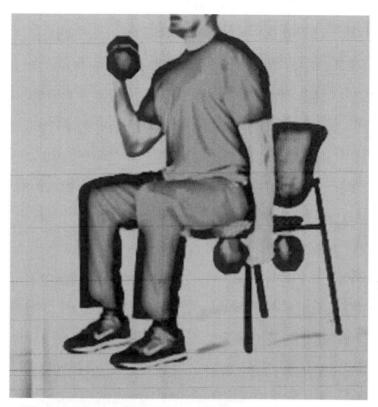

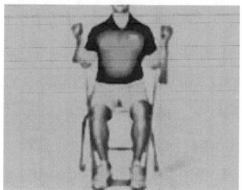

Difficulty: Easy

Sets/Reps: 3/12

Time: 4 Minutes

Instructions:

- Pick up some weights or a fitness band.

- Slide the band under your chair seat or sit on it till the resistant band length is equal to your body.

- Sit in a chair comfortably with your hips back.

- Be sure your back is properly supported by the chair's backrest.

- Hold your abs and low back in. Put your chest out.

- Hold both arms out to the sides of the body, allowing them to hang naturally with the palms of both hands facing forward while maintaining the elbows tucked in (at the sides of your body).

- Then, curl both arms toward the chest, from the sides of the body to the front of the shoulders (the senior doesn't have to touch their hands to their shoulders for a full range of motion).

- Slowly return both forearms to the beginning position while maintaining tension.

Triceps

Although the triceps don't play a significant role in picking up objects, elderly citizens who are self-conscious about hanging underarm skin (whether due to excess skin or fat) and who want to tone this region might benefit greatly from triceps workouts.

Isolated Triceps Extensions

Difficulty: Medium

Sets/Reps: 3/12

Time: 7 Minutes

If you've been working on establishing shoulder motion, then this exercise will come much more naturally to you.

Instructions:

- To begin, hold a dumbbell.

- Sit in a chair comfortably with your hips back.

- Make sure your back is properly supported by the chair's backrest.

- Keep your core tight. Put your chest out.

- Maintain a "V" shape by keeping both elbows up in front of your body with one hand lowered and placed behind the head. Support the forearm slightly below the elbow with your free hand.

- Do not let the assisting hand move from its current position. The palm holding the dumbbell should be facing upward.

- Extend the arm that is holding the dumbbell above your head.

- Deliberately return the forearm to its initial resting position.

- It should be repeated for both arms.

Chest Press With Band

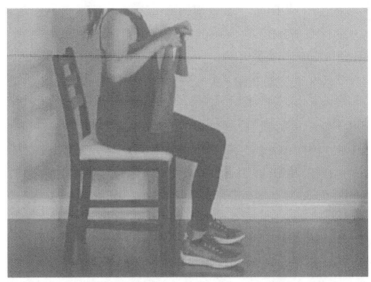

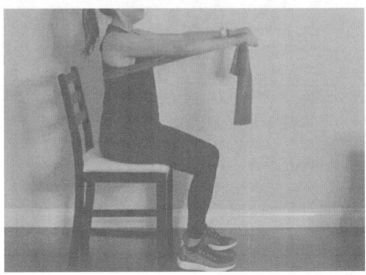

Difficulty: Easy

Sets/Reps: 3/10

Time: 6 Minutes

Instructions:

- Sit tall on a chair with the band's ends in each hand, and wrap it around your back.

- The band should be placed inside your arms.

- To begin, press your fists out so that you can feel the tension in the band.

- Picture yourself hitting forward with both fists.

- Slowly throw out a punch and bring your fists back into your chest.

- Perform 10 repetitions.

Pull Aparts

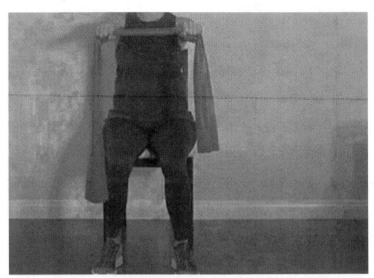

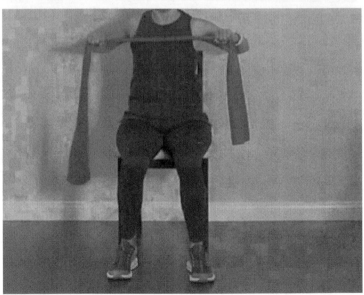

Difficulty: Easy

Sets/Reps: 3/10

Time: 6 Minutes

Instructions:

- Sit tall on a chair

- To begin, Grab the band and lift it to your front, should be level & hip-width apart

- Bring your elbows back and squeeze your shoulder blades together.

- You should feel the band pulling apart.

- Get back to the beginning

- Perform 10 repetitions.

Tricep Extension With Band

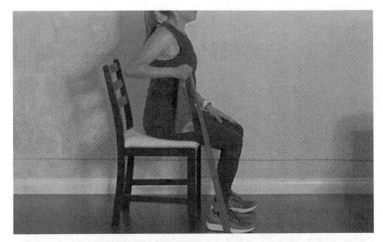

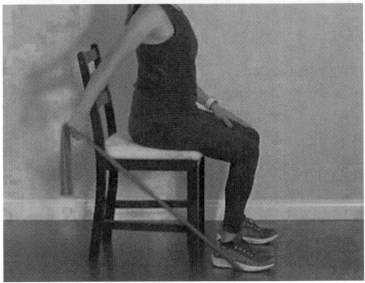

Difficulty: Easy

Sets/Reps: 3/5

Time: 5 Minutes

Instructions;

- Sit tall on a chair

- Plant your right foot firmly on the band.

- To begin, stretch the band so that it is firm and pull your right arm back so that your upper arm is slightly elevated and your elbow is pointed toward the back of the room.

- With the upper arms stationary, slowly flex the elbow and extend the arm.

- Perform 5 repetitions.

- Switch sides and repeat.

Core Exercises For Seniors

All that we do throughout the day revolves around the core. When we're upright, walking, squatting, or even sitting, our abdominal muscles are working hard. Poor posture can cause muscle stress and other issues, therefore it's important to engage our core muscles when standing or sitting.

Seated Knee-to-Chest

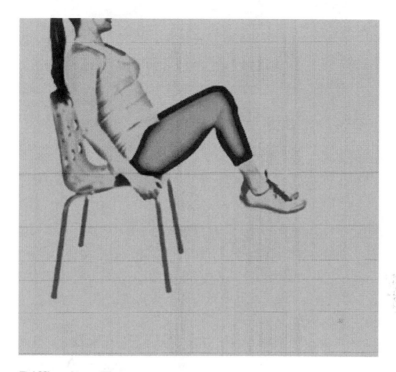

Difficulty: Easy

Sets/Reps: 2-3/8-12

Time: 4 Minutes

Instructions:

- Sit at the chair's edge without feeling like you're going to fall over.

- Maintain a straight back while contracting the core muscles (abs & lumbar). Put your chest out.

- Maintain your balance by placing both hands on the chair's arms and gripping the seat.

- Put both feet a significant distance in front of the body, and then point the toes of both feet toward the ceiling. Both feet ought to be pointing in a direction that is diagonal to your hips.

- In slow motion, bring both legs in toward your body while bending your knees. Try to get both knees as near to your chest as you can.

- Repeat the motion in reverse to return to the initial position.

- Keep in mind that you can perform these moves independently on each leg if you prefer. Before you lift, ensure sure the other leg is securely placed on the ground.

Seated Side Bends

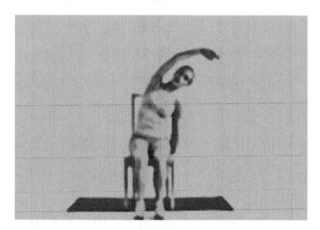

Difficulty: Easy

Sets/Reps: 3/12

Time: 4 Minutes

Instructions:

- Sit down comfortably in a chair, knees bent and your feet firmly planted on the floor.

- Lift your right-hand overhead and bend it over. Let your left arm dangle at your side.

- Do not slouch or slump back in the chair; instead, maintain an upright posture.

- Inhale. carefully Gently bend at the waist and bring the left hand toward the ground as you exhale.

- Maintain an open chest position and gently draw your right elbow behind you to feel a stretch on the right side of your body.

- Breathe in and return to the beginning position. Switch sides and repeat.

Extended Leg Raises

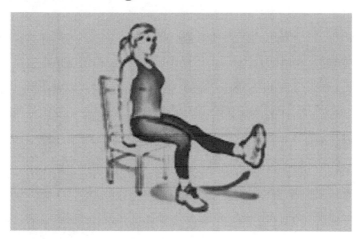

Difficulty: Medium

Sets/Reps: 3/12

Time: 4 Minutes

Instructions:

- Sit comfortably on the chair's edge without feeling like you're going to fall over.

- Hold a firm core (abs & lumbar) and a straight back. Proudly expose one's chest.

- Maintain your balance by placing both hands on the chair's arms and gripping the seat.

- Extend your legs straight in front of you and point your toes up. Put both feet in a diagonal position to the hips.

- Raise one leg to the top of its range of motion (the optimal range should end at the hips) while keeping the core stationery. The opposite leg will remain in the initial posture throughout.

- Bring the leg down to the starting position slowly, and then do the opposing leg.

- Kicking both legs counts as one "rep."

- Keep in mind that you can do this exercise by focusing on just one leg at a time. When elevating one leg, ensure sure the other is securely planted on the ground.

Abdominal Lean - (abdominals)

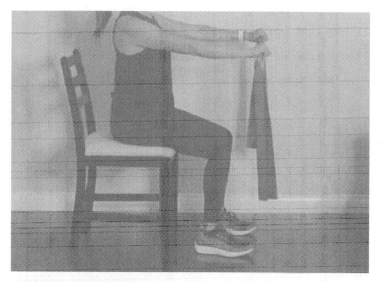

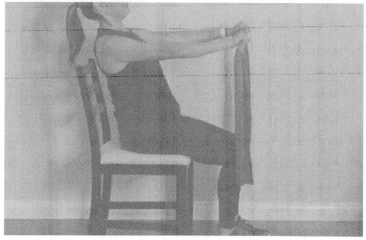

Difficulty: Easy

Sets/Reps: 3/5

Time: 5 Minutes

Instructions:

- Sit in the center of your chair, leaving enough room behind you.

- Place your feet hip-width apart on the floor.

- Hold the band firmly while maintaining shoulder distance and height

- Engage your core and sit up straight.

- Maintain a straight alignment of the head, neck, & spine.

- Lean back and feel the tension in your front abdominals.

- Get back up

- Perform 5 repetitions of 3 sets

Leg Kicks

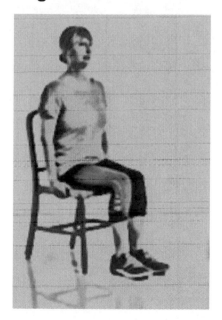

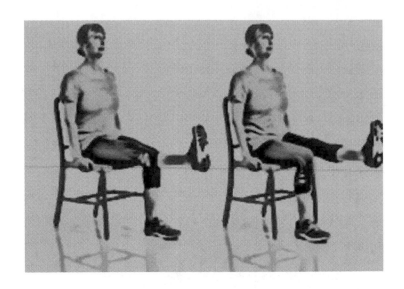

Difficulty: Advance

Sets/Reps: 3/12

Time: 5 Minutes

In terms of movement, this exercise is quite similar to extended leg lifts.

Instructions:

- Sit comfortably on the chair's edge without feeling like you're going to fall over.

- Hold a firm core (abs & lumbar) and a straight back.

- Maintain your balance by placing both hands on the chair's arms and gripping the seat.

- Start by extending your legs and pointing your toes straight in front. Put both feet in a diagonal position to your hips. Lean back carefully as you bring both feet forward to steady yourself as you make the move.

- Raise one leg as high as possible, ideally till it's parallel to your hips, without shifting the center of your body.

- Slowly return the leg to the initial position, and then repeat with the opposite leg. Imagine the person doing this action while swimming and kicking their legs in the water; this is a helpful mental image to keep in mind when performing the movement.

- One "rep" is equal to one kick on each leg.

- To increase the difficulty of this routine, you should resist the need to put your feet down until the workout is over. This action can be performed individually on each leg. Before lifting, be sure the other leg is firmly placed on the ground

Modified Planks

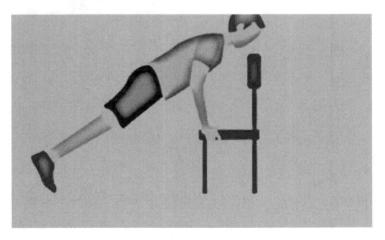

Difficulty: Advance

Sets/Reps: 3/30 Seconds

Time: 4 Minutes

The plank is a great workout for strengthening your core at any age. This workout challenges your core, which forces you to maintain balance and stability. One of the many benefits of training with this motion is improved posture while seated.

Instructions:

- Stand straight and face the chair.

- Hold the chair's sides with both hands. Slightly bend your elbow and move your feet behind till your body is in a diagonal position to the chair.

- Keep your back straight and your buttocks down. Maintain a straight line from your shoulder to your heel. When a senior feel resistance or stress in their core, this indicates that they are in the appropriate position.

- Hold this position for thirty seconds (or for as long as is comfortable without causing pain), and then go into a standing or seated position to give yourself a little break.

- Repeat 2 to 3 times.

- Tip: The chair will be more stable if it is pushed up against a wall.

Tummy Twists

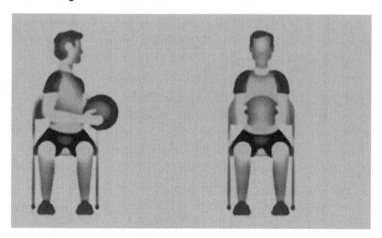

Difficulty: Medium

Sets/Reps: 3/10

Time: 5 Minutes

This is an excellent spinal extension exercise that works the entire abdominal region. If you want to feel the full effect on your abs, try doing this with a medicine ball or comparable object.

Instructions:

- Get a medicine ball (or a similar object).

- Place yourself toward the outer edge of the chair for more legroom. Maintain a firm abdominal and low back core. Put your chest out.

- The medicine ball should be held in front of your body with both hands, and elbows bent.

- Raise the ball off the lap by a few inches and spin your upper body to your right while maintaining the position in your front.

- First, rotate your body to the middle, then to the left, and finally back to the center.

- One complete rotation counts as one "rep."

Seated Forward Roll-ups

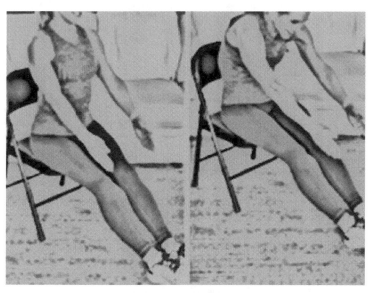

Difficulty: Medium

Sets/Reps: 3/8

Time: 5 Minutes

Instruction:

- Sit tall in a chair, your legs stretch out with your heels on the ground and your feet flexed to your face.

- Extend your hand out in your front. Maintain a good posture by sitting up straight and without slouching or leaning back on the chair.

- Start bringing your chin closer to your chest. While maintaining your legs still and your abs tight, exhale and roll your entire torso up & over. Try to reach down to your toes.

- Once you are unable to push any further, breathe in as you bring yourself back up beginning position.

- Repeat with gentle movement. Don't rely on momentum; instead, engage your abs to raise & lower.

Leg/Hip/Thigh, Harmstring Exercises For Seniors

We utilize our legs to get around daily unless we're in a wheelchair or some other similar situation. Using our legs entails a wide range of activities, from standing to walking to running to climbing stairs to bending over to pick something up. Maintaining our leg muscle mass as we become older is a very important physical consideration.

However, if an elderly person has a knee injury or has recently had knee surgery, activities such as jogging, running, & climbing stairs can be very taxing on the body. However, doing exercises while seated can help maintain leg strength & endurance without putting unnecessary strain on the joints.

Get the proper footwear before beginning the following routines. It may come as a surprise, but the shoes you wear during exercise are crucial. Even if a loved one is not jogging, trekking, or carrying heavy weights, they will still want shoes with cushioning (for comfort) & stability (for support). The flat soles of shoes can help prevent the wearer's knees & back from caving inward toward the center of their body during squatting-like movements.

Quick Tip:

After having knee surgery, you will need to work on regaining your range of motion. Roll out your toes by placing your heels on top of balls that are 8 to 12 inches in diameter. Slowly bring the ball back towards your heels until you've completed a full rollout. Your knee will gradually regain its range of motion.

Sit-to-Stands

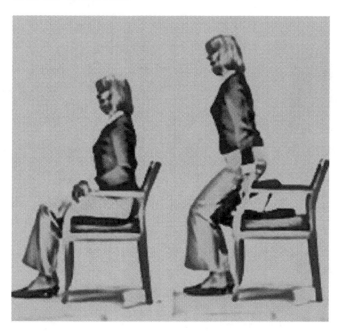

Difficulty: Easy

Sets/Reps: 3/12

Time: 5 Minutes

To begin, the elderly person should just use their body weight for this exercise. If individuals find the exercise to be too simple, even though their bodies enjoy performing it, they can increase the difficulty by adding weight, such as a medicine ball.

If individuals find the exercise to be too simple, even though their bodies enjoy performing it, they can increase the difficulty by adding weight, such as a medicine ball.

Instruction:

- Comfortably position yourself toward the chair's edge.

- Hold your abs and low back in. Put your chest out.

- Make sure that your toes are pointing slightly forward to your sides; place your hands at your front, in a position that is comfortable for you, to maintain balance.

- Gently rise from your seat until you are standing. When rising from a seated position to a standing one should make sure their knees are not folding inward; rather, they should be extending outward from the middle of the body. With this move, you should not use your knees to push yourself up into a standing position, but rather your hips.

- To return to the starting position, sit back down and double-check the positioning of your knees.

Note: Squeezing the glutes (butt) together as you rise to your feet is an effective way to increase glute engagement and kick-start muscle training.

Modified Squats

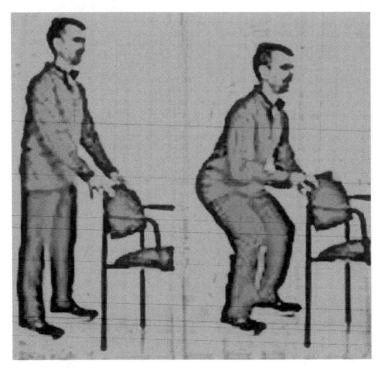

Difficulty: Medium

Sets/Reps: 2/8

Time: 5 Minutes

Squatting is widely recognized as one of the best exercises for people of all ages. Unfortunately, a regular squat is beyond the capabilities of some people, and that's when outside help comes in handy.

Instructions:

- Stand at the back of the chair. Take a step backward from the chair.

- Directly align the body with the center of the chair. Extend your arms in front of you.

- Place both feet hip-width apart and straight under the body.

- Toes should be pointed forward or outward slightly from the center of your body.

- While maintaining the position of your knees behind your toes (do not allow them to cross over the toes), bend both knees, release the hips, and lower the buttocks toward the ground. Keep a close eye on both knees to make sure they don't cave in toward the midline of the body, and instead, drive them outward.

- You should halt in a squat position and then push yourself back up to a standing posture.

- To prevent the chair from shifting, please prop the front of it against a wall. You can also lay your hands straight on top of the chair for stability if the back is high.

Heel Slides

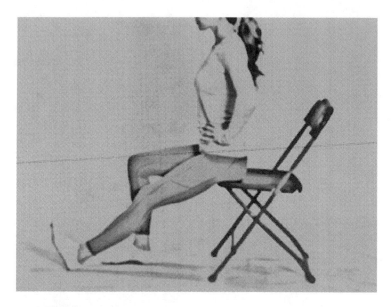

Difficulty: Easy

Sets/Reps: 2/8

Time: 6 Minutes

This workout may not be suitable for an elderly person who has severe knee discomfort right now due to the pressure it puts on the joints. If a senior has knee pain, minimal pressure should be applied so as not to irritate the joint. Get a blanket or a towel and put it down in front of the chair to prevent scratching the floor.

Instruction:

- Comfortably sit toward the chair's edge.

- Maintain a tight core by contracting the abs & the lumbar. Put your chest out.

- Maintain your balance by placing both hands on the chair's arms and gripping the seat.

- Stretch one of your legs out and ensure that your toes are pointed forward.

- The foot of the extended leg should be angled diagonally to the hips. Put your foot on top of the blanket or whatever you're using. You should keep your other leg bent naturally, with your foot flat on the floor and near to your body.

- Maintain a flat foot with the extended leg, press against the ground, and slowly drag the foot toward the body till it reaches the flexed position of the opposite leg.

- Maintaining pressure, return the leg to its starting position while extending it backward.

- A single repetition is achieved by completing the whole movement, which consists of pulling and then pushing the foot back to the beginning position.

Seated Calf Raises

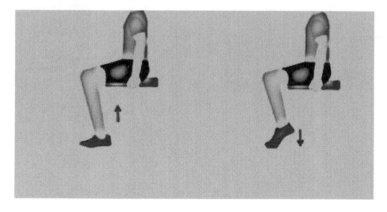

Difficulty: Easy

Sets/Reps: 3/25

Time: 6 Minutes

Calf raises may be helpful for seniors who are experiencing tightness in their calves & finding it difficult to squat.

Instructions:

- Sit on a chair comfortably with your hips back.

- Make sure your back is properly supported by the chair's backrest.

- Maintain a tight core by contracting the abs and the lumbar. Put your chest out.

- To maintain balance, put your hands on the chair's arms and grab the seat.

- Maintain a 90-degree angle between the chair and both legs. Keep both of your feet firmly planted on the ground.

- Carefully push your feet' heels upward, using your toes to lift the heels.

- Bring your feet back to their original positions.

- Do at least 20 repetitions of this exercise to feel the "burn" in your calves.

Those who find the exercise too simple while using only their body weight might add resistance by placing a medicine ball or similar weight of comparable worth towards the outer border of their lap (almost to the knees). Another option is to raise one or both feet off the ground by 3 to 4 inches to increase your range of motion.

Point and Flex - ankles, feet, calves

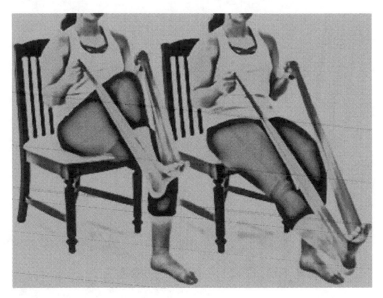

Difficulty: Medium

Sets/Reps: 3/5

Time: 5 Minutes

Instructions:

- Start by using your hands to hold the ends of the band.

- Place the ball of your right foot inside the band's loop.

- Check that the band has tension when your toes are pointed.

- Flex your foot, that's one rep.

- Perform five on the right, then five on the left.

Leg Press - (thighs, hamstrings, glutes)

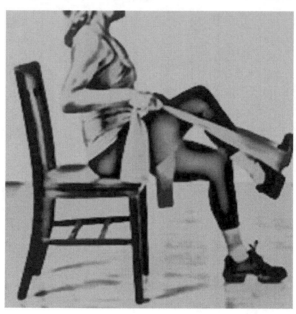

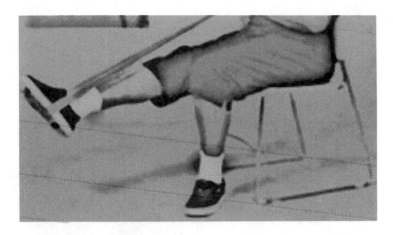

Difficulty: Easy

Sets/Reps: 3/8

Time: 5 Minutes

Instructions:

- To do this, grab the band and hold both ends.

- Place the ball of your right foot inside the band's loop.

- Now, carefully bend your knee & then straighten them out.

- Switch sides and repeat.

Knee Extensions

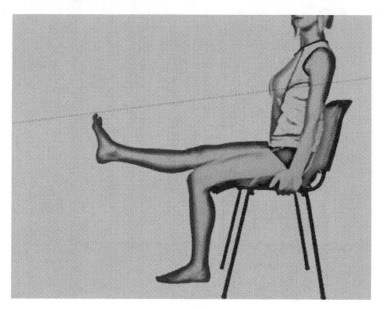

Difficulty: Easy

Sets/Reps: 3/12

Time: 6 Minutes

Instructions:

- Sit on the chair comfortably with your hips back.

- Be sure your back is properly supported by the chair's backrest.

- Maintain a tight core by contracting the abs & the lumbar. Put your chest out.

- You should keep both hands on the chair's edges and hold the seat for support.

- Maintain a 90-degree angle between the chair and both legs.

- Lift and hold one leg in the air in front of you at full length. Maintain the initial position of the other leg for maximum stability.

- Carefully bring the extended leg back to its beginning position.

- Repeat for the other leg to make one set.

Front Thigh Leg Lift

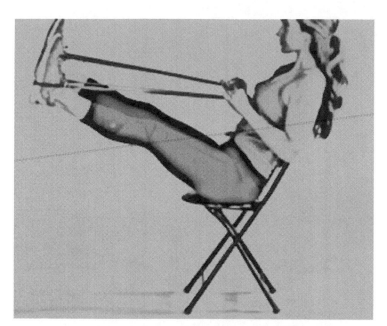

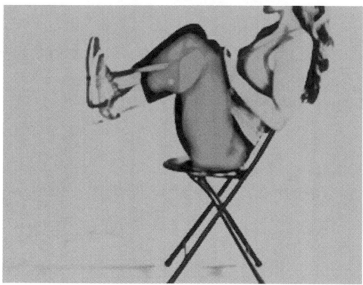

Difficulty: Medium

Sets/Reps: 3/8

Time: 5 Minutes

Instructions:

- Begin by holding the band's end with each hand.

- Place the ball of your right foot inside the band's loop.

- Raise your leg gently, toes pointing upwards.

- Slowly bring the leg down.

Hip Opener -(hips, thighs)

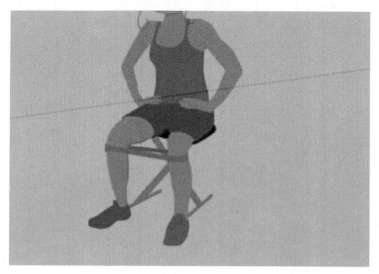

Difficulty: Easy

Sets/Reps: 3/5

Time: 5 Minutes

Instructions:

- Place the band over the top of the thighs in an even manner on both the right & left sides.

- Cross the band's ends underneath your thighs.

- Take hold of the ends of the bands with both hands and position your arms so that they form a 90-degree angle to your body.

- Move out & into the right for five reps

- Repeat to the left.

Squat

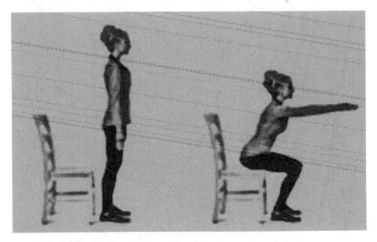

Difficulty: Easy

Sets/Reps: 3/12

Time: 4 Minutes

Instructions:

- Stand with your feet shoulder-width apart and your toes facing forward while backing your chair.

- While keeping the chest raised, bend the knees to sit the hips back & down. Just tap your butt on the seat of the chair softly.

- Raise to your starting position and repeat

Seated Hamstring Stretch With A Strap

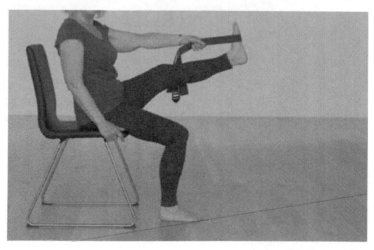

Difficulty: Easy

Sets/Reps: 3/10

Time: 6 Minutes

Your calves & hamstrings will feel a nice stretch, and you'll engage your abs, which will help you maintain your balance.

Instructions:

- Create a loop with a belt or strap and slip it over your right foot. The strap should be held in the right hand, while the left hand can rest comfortably on the chair's edge for stability if necessary.

- Begin straightening and lifting your right leg while keeping your spine as straight as possible. You are free to keep your knee bent if it makes you feel more comfortable.

- While you are in the pose, you can improve circulation by pointing your toes and flexing your feet several times. This will pump your calves.

- If you want a little more of a challenge, you can loosen the strap a little bit so that you have to use the muscles in your hip flexors to keep the leg raised.

- If you want a little more of a challenge, you can loosen the strap a little bit so that you have to use the muscles in your hip flexors to keep your leg raised.

- After you've taken a couple of deep breaths, put your right foot back on the ground. Stop to focus on how your body feels before switching sides.

Neck Turns

Difficulty: Easy

Sets/Reps: 5/20-30 Seconds

Time: 5 Minutes

A sore and stiff neck is one of the most unpleasant conditions. If a senior has trouble sleeping due to neck pain or can't turn their head freely, stretching may help.

Instructions:

- Comfortably sit on the chair with your hips back.

- Make sure your back is properly supported by the chair's backrest.

Maintain a straight spine & an upright back to stabilize the core. Make sure you plant both feet firmly on the ground.

- While maintaining this position, slowly turn your head to the right or left until you feel a little stretch. Hold for the full 30 seconds if possible.

- Change directions when the allotted time has passed.

- Do this in both directions as many times as you feel is comfortable, usually between three and five times.

Seated Backbend

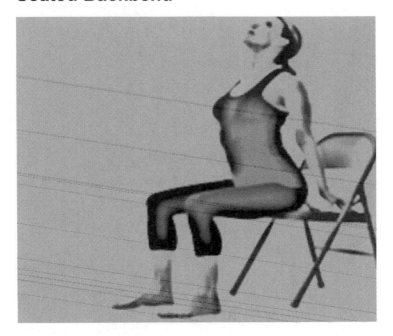

Difficulty: Easy

Sets/Reps: 5/10-20 Seconds

Time: 4 Minutes

This stretch targets the lower back, neck, and chest, relieving discomfort and tightness throughout the entire body.

Instructions:

- Sit comfortably on the chair's edge. Maintain a straight spine & an upright back to stabilize the core. Always keep both feet firmly planted on the ground. Maintain this position with your hips & lower body.

- Put your hands on your hIps.

- First, slowly arch your back inward while pulling your stomach outward, and then lean back using just your upper body.

- Until you feel a good stretch, extend your back in this position.

- Hold for 10 to 20 seconds and then come back to the beginning position.

- Repeat the pattern 3 to 5 times, or as often as is comfortable.

Glute stretch

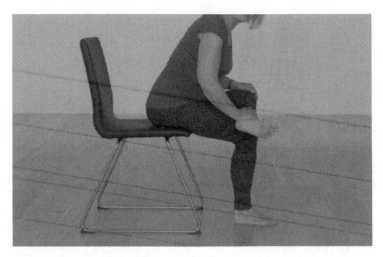

Difficulty: Easy

Sets/Reps: 3/5

Time: 4 Minutes

The piriformis & gluteal muscles will both benefit from this move.

Instructions:

- To begin, lift your right foot some inches off the ground, grab hold of your knee, & make circles with it; perform this movement 3 times in each direction. This will serve as the beginning of some light mobility exercises for the hip joint.

- Put your left foot over your right knee & move the left knee back and forth a few times. If you are unable to raise your ankle to your knee, you can try crossing the ankle in front of your shin & resting the foot on a block if you have one. This is an alternative to bringing your ankle up to your knee.

- From here, extend your spine while inhaling and fold forward while exhaling. Don't push yourself beyond your limits.

Seated Overhead Stretch

Difficulty: Easy

Sets/Reps: 5/20 Seconds

Time: 4 Minutes

Instructions:

- Sit comfortably on the chair's edge. Maintain a straight spine and an upright back to stabilize the core.
- Make sure you plant both feet firmly on the ground. Maintain this position with your hips & lower body.

- Raise your hands slowly over your head and interlock your hands.

- Slowly arch your back inward, pulling the stomach out, causing the abdomen to stretch.

- Hold for 10-20 seconds, then return to the beginning position.

- Perform the exercise three to five times, or until you feel fatigued.

Seated Hero's pose

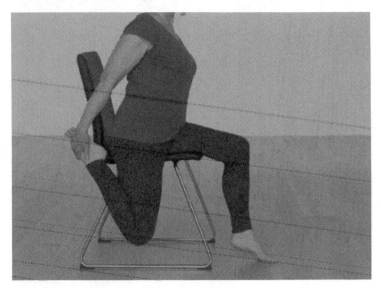

Difficulty: Easy

Sets/Reps: 3/5

Time: 3 Minutes

Instructions:

The large front thigh quadriceps muscles are worked on in the hero's pose, as well as the hip flexors, psoas included. Because these muscles frequently become tight when we sit for long periods, this position is also useful for people whose jobs require them to sit for long periods, such as those who work at desks all day.

Instructions:

- Move to the right side of your chair so that your right leg is hanging off the edge. Use your left hand to grasp the chair's armrest.

- Lean to your left while bending the right knee and taking hold of the foot with your right hand. If it is more convenient for you, you can wrap a strap over your foot at this point.
- Draw your heel up toward your buttock. You should feel a stretch at the front of your thigh.

- Release a little of the pressure on your foot if your knee starts to ache more.

Seated Side Stretch

Difficulty: Medium

Sets/Reps: 5/10-20 Seconds

Time: 8 Minutes

Instructions:

- Sit comfortably on the chair's edge. Maintain a straight spine and an upright back to stabilize the core.

- Make sure you plant both feet firmly on the ground. Maintain this steady position with the hips & lower body.

- For balance, using your right hand, hold the right side of your seat.

- Raise your left hand in the air so that it forms a spoon or an elongated "C" over your head.

- At the same time, rotate your upper body to the right in a controlled manner without bringing your stomach in toward your spine (keep it tight).

- Hold for 10-20 seconds, then switch sides.

- Perform three to five times on each side, or until fatigue sets in.

Seated Hip Stretch

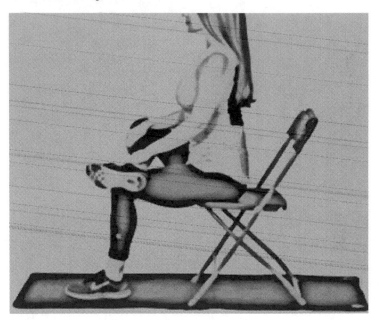

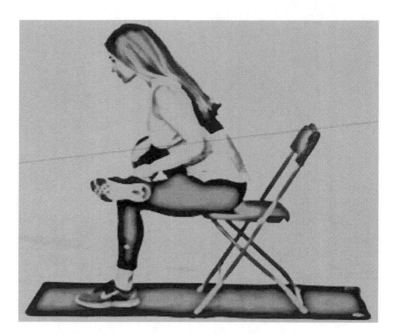

Difficulty: Easy

Sets/Reps: 5/20 Seconds

Time: 8 Minutes

Hips play a significant role in our daily lives. If a senior is slouching, has difficulty moving their legs at the hips, feels like they are waddling when they walk or has a pattern of pain in the general area of their hips, they may find that this stretch is beneficial.

Instructions:

- Comfortably sit in a chair,

- Maintain a straight spine and an upright back to stabilize the core. Make sure you plant both feet firmly on the ground.

- Place one leg over the other so that your legs form a triangle. Make sure the ankle of the crossed leg is past the ankle on the other leg.

- In a slow, controlled motion, bend forward from the shoulders while keeping your core firm and your spine straight. If you encounter any resistance from your glutes or hips, you should stop.

- Maintain this position for ten to twenty seconds, and then switch sides.

- Repeat three to five times or as many times as is comfortable, per leg.

Chair Cat-Cow

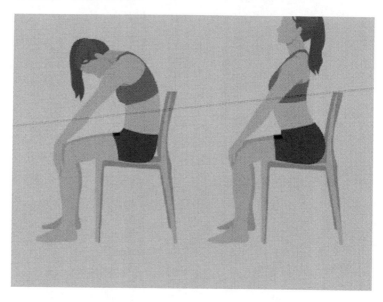

Difficulty: Easy

Reps: 10

Time: 2 Minutes

Instructions:

- Sit tall on a chair with a straight back and feet firmly planted on the ground. Hands-on knees or thighs.

- Inhale to lift the spine and rotate the shoulders back & down, bringing the blades of your shoulders together on your back. This is the cow pose

- Exhale and round the spine, bringing the chin to the chest, allowing the shoulders & head to move forward. Taking the cat pose.

- For the next five breaths, alternate between the cow and cat positions.

Chair Raised Hands Pose

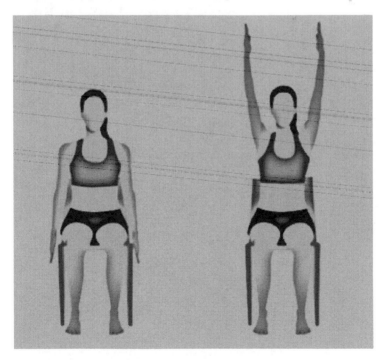

Difficulty: Easy

Reps: 10

Time: 2 Minutes

Instructions:

- Lift your arms upward as you inhale.

- Keep your shoulders down and back and your rib cage up so that they're aligned with your hips.

- Place your sit bones firmly in the chair seat, then raise yourself from there.

Chair Forward Bend

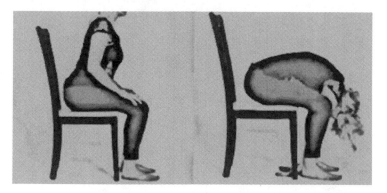

Difficulty: Easy

Reps: 10

Time: 2 Minutes

Instructions:

- Exhale and bend forward over your legs. If the hands can reach the ground, let them rest there. Let your head hang low.

- Inhale as you bring your arms back up above your head. Move with the breath as you move through this action numerous times, alternating between having your arms elevated and being in a folded forward position.

Chair Extended Side Angle

Difficulty: Easy

Reps: 10

Time: 1 Minute

Instructions:

- Keep your body folded once you've made your final forward bend. Bring the fingertips of your left hand to the floor on the outside of your left foot. If you're having trouble getting your left hand to the floor, try putting a block under it or bringing it to your left knee and twisting from there.

- While inhaling, rotate to the right and bring your right arm up to the ceiling as you open your chest and look up at the ceiling.

- This is the chair-based alternative to the extended side angle pose. For a few deep breaths, hold. While exhaling, lower your right arm.

- Carry out the same move with your right arm lowered and your left arm raised.

Chair Pigeon

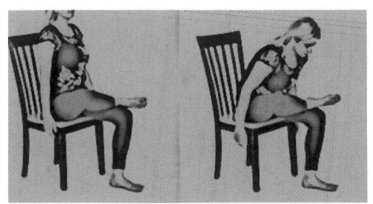

Difficulty: Easy

Reps: 5

Time: 40 seconds

Instructions:

- BrIng yourself up to sit. Raise the right ankle to relax on the left thigh, ensuring that your knee is in line with the ankle.

- Take three to five deep breaths while holding this chair pigeon.

- If you want a deeper stretch, you can forward bend. Repeat the process with your left leg.

Chair Eagle

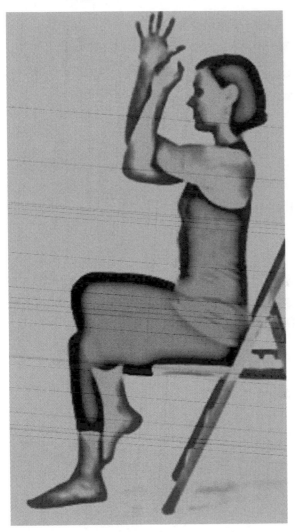

Difficulty: Easy

Reps: 5

Time: 40 seconds

Instructions:

- The eagle pose is achieved by crossing the right thigh over the left. Wrap your right foot around your left calf as tightly as you can.

- At the elbow, interlace your left and right arms. Bend the elbows & bring the palms together.

- Raise the elbows and move the shoulders down and back. Hold for 3 to 5 breaths.

- Continue on the opposite side.

Seated Single-Leg Extensions

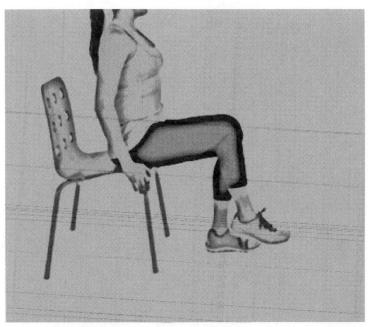

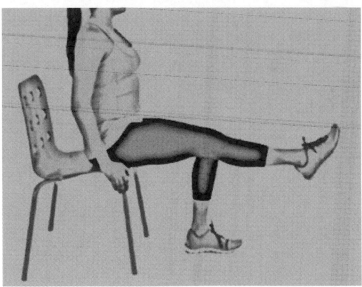

Difficulty: Easy

Sets/Reps: 3/12

Time: 4 Minutes

Instructions:

- Sit comfortably in a chair with a straight back, feet firmly planted on the floor & grab the seat side.

- While keeping one foot firmly on the ground and the upper body still, extend the other leg until it is parallel to the ground.

- Bring your foot back down to the ground by bending your knee. Repeat as many times as necessary, then move to the opposite leg.

Chair Spinal Twist

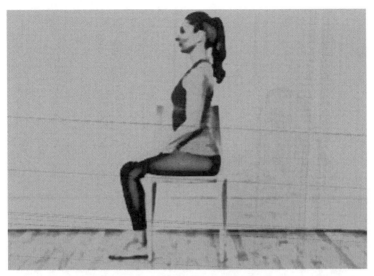

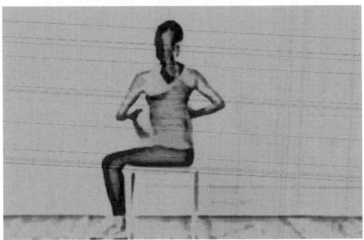

Difficulty: Easy

Reps: 5

Time: 1 minute

Instructions:

- Sit sideways on the chair while gazing towards your left. To do a spinal twist, rotate your upper body to the left while maintaining a firm grip on the chair's back.

- Hold this position for five breaths, lengthening your spine on the inhale and twisting it on the exhale.

- Turn your legs to the right and repeat the twist.

Chair Warrior I

Difficulty: Easy

Reps: 5

Time: 40 seconds

Instructions

- Next, maintain your right leg's position over the chair's edge as you swing your left leg behind.

- Place the bottom of your left foot on the ground in a position that is about parallel to the chair's seat, and then straighten the left leg.

- On an inhale, get into the warrior I position by raising your arms overhead while keeping the torso looking over the right leg. Count to three before releasing.

Chair Warrior II

Difficulty: Easy

Reps: 5

Time: 40 seconds

Instructions

- Exhale and spread your arms wide, bringing the right arm forward & the left one back.

- To get your body in line with the front of the chair, you'll need to rotate your torso to the left and draw your left hip back behind you.

- Hold the position of Warrior II for five deep breaths while you cast your gaze out over your right fingertips.

Reverse Warrior

Difficulty: Easy

Reps: 3

Time: 20 seconds

Instructions:

- To accomplish a reverse warrior pose, exhale and bring your left arm down to your left knee while simultaneously reaching your right arm as high as you can towards the ceiling. Count to three before releasing.

- Move both legs to the chair's front before sitting on the left side of the chair facing left and performing the three warrior postures on the left side of the body.

Chair Savasana

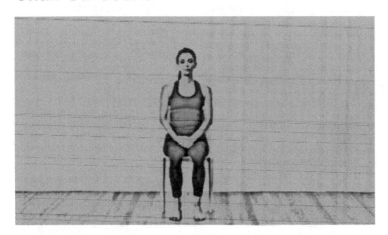

Difficulty: Easy

Time: 1 minute

Instructions:

After your workout, take a few minutes to sit quietly with your eyes closed and your hands in your lap. Your body will be able to fully benefit from the exercises you just completed as you relax in this seated savasana and prepare for the rest of the day

Conclusion

Elderly individuals should never push too hard when performing any of the aforementioned activities; doing so could result in injury or worse. They should not force their body to do the exercises if it is having difficulty doing so. When we push ourselves physically, our bodies provide feedback on whether an action is beneficial or harmful. The muscles in our body are like a chain; if one link is weak, the whole thing will be affected.

Nutrition should be considered by both the seniors and their caretakers as they attempt to establish a healthier routine that includes regular exercise. Consuming nutritious meals and snacks regularly is not only important but also has the potential to increase one's energy levels, which is especially beneficial for elderly people who often struggle with fatigue.

Disclaimer: This information is provided solely for educational and informational reasons. It is not designed to provide medical advice, nor is it meant to substitute for the medical advice or treatment that one would receive from their physician. It is strongly recommended that anyone who reads this discuss any specific concerns or questions they may have regarding their health with their physician or another appropriately trained health expert.

Made in United States
Orlando, FL
10 August 2023

35953104R00072